CORNELL UNIVERSITY COLLEGE OF VETERINARY MEDICINE

The Well-Behaved Cat: How to Change Your Cat's *Bad* Habits

Editors:

Katherine A. Houpt, VMD, PhD
Director, Cornell Animal Behavior Clinic

James R. Richards, DVM
Director, Cornell Feline Health Center

With Advice From Fred Kent, DVM

A Special Report From CatWatch®

This publication is not intended to give individual veterinary advice or diagnosis. Readers should consult their veterinarian with specific questions about or for specific diagnosis of their cat's health and behavior. We regret that we cannot respond to individual inquiries about feline health matters.

Express written permission is required to reproduce, in any manner, the contents of this publication, either in full or in part. For more information write: Permissions, Torstar Publications, Inc., 99 Hawley Lane, Stratford, CT 06614.

© 1999 Torstar Publications, Inc.
® is a trademark of Torstar Publications, Inc.

Contents

	Introduction	1
CHAPTER 1	Socialization, Problem Behaviors, and Normal Social Behavior	3
	Critical or Sensitive Periods	3
	Problem Behaviors	7
	Normal Social Behaviors	15
CHAPTER 2	Grooming: Normal and Destructive	19
	Normal Grooming	19
	When Good Grooming Affects Your Furniture	20
CHAPTER 3	Housesoiling	25
	Eliminative Behavior Development	25
	What Cats Do	26
	Why They Do It—Spraying	30
	Why They Do It—Inappropriate Urination and Defecation	33
	How to Resolve Problems—Spraying	38
	How to Resolve Problems—Inappropriate Urination and Defecation	41
	Summary	49
	Recommended Resources on Cat Behavior	51

Introduction

Many people think that the full panoply of cat behavior encompasses napping and eating—and maybe a desultory stretch. There are times, as a cat owner, when you might wish that were the case. Cats can make it very plain to you that you share your abode with them, and that they are forces with whom you must reckon. They have a formidable array of behaviors that never let you forget who is in charge. Some of these behaviors may well drive you to distraction—and, in some cases, may lead you to the desire to abandon the cat.

Because of their independent nature and natural meticulousness in grooming and personal hygiene, cats can be the perfect companion for people who do not wish to invest a great deal of time and effort in acclimating their companion to the household. Because of their small size and usually gentle natures, cats do not pose a potential threat to their owners.

However, not all cats are "problem-free": At one time or another, cat owners may encounter one or a number of feline misbehaviors. One common form of misbehavior is inappropriate elimination (urination or defecation). Instead of using the litter box, the cat chooses to eliminate elsewhere in the house. Alternatively, the cat may scratch the furniture or act aggressively toward another cat. It is even possible, although less common, for the cat to be aggressive to humans. In rarer cases, the cat may behave in even more destructive or irritating ways—such as tearing up papers, throwing items onto the floor, or even pulling wallpaper off walls—or may meow constantly. While these activities are within the range of normal feline behavior, this is no comfort to the cat owner who must replace the furniture or who is kept up all night by Fluffy's meowing.

The following Special Report on cat misbehaviors (and good behaviors) will help you and your beloved cat change the unwelcome feline habits that nearly drive you to distraction.

Chapter 1

Socialization, Problem Behaviors, and Normal Social Behavior

Critical or Sensitive Periods

Critical or sensitive periods are the times during development when certain behavioral interactions must occur to result in development of a particular kind of behavior. In cats, the critical period for development of friendliness to people is between the ages of two to seven weeks, beginning just about the time when their eyelids have totally opened and they are beginning to see more clearly, and when play behavior begins. Thus, kittens handled by people during that time are more likely to become friendly to humans. If different people handle them once they're about four or five weeks old, the kittens will be less afraid of strangers. Some cats also start out with a genetic complement that may make them more friendly to humans: If the father has genes that make him friendly, the kittens are more likely to inherit the trait of friendliness. Mothers who carry genes for friendliness may also pass these genes on to their kittens.

Of course, that leaves us with two situations over which we have little or no control. We rarely know who fathered any litter of kittens, and it's rare that any but a purebred cat comes from someone's home. Thus, when we adopt a cat from a shelter, from the street, or from the veterinarian's office, we know nothing of the cat's life during its critical period and are just taking a leap of faith.

Cats who have not had opportunities to be handled by humans during the critical period will hiss at any approaching human—even while they are very young. There is some evidence that kittens who are handled daily may be able to learn better than those who are not.

Cats who do not have opportunities to play as kittens—for example, those who are abandoned by humans or their mothers when they are very young—do not ever seem to be able to respond to signals to play. Development of play behavior begins when the cat is about two weeks old and continues until the cat is four months old. At that point, play behavior decreases, although some cats are willing to play throughout their lives.

Why are developmental periods so important? We know that neurological development of young animals requires stimuli that cause neurons (nerve cells) to form synapses (connections) with other neurons. Synapses help form the neuronal pathways on which messages for certain behaviors will travel. Without stimulation, such synapses do not develop.

Do's and Don'ts of Socializing

It is important to expose the kittens to both adults and children during the socialization period, because their still-developing eyesight fixes on a vague form and size rather than a definitive image. Thus, adults and children will look different to a kitten.

Avoid roughhousing when playing, or rough handling during interactions with the kittens, as they will only learn to fear and avoid you, or conversely, to become aggressive toward you. The kittens will develop the same aversive behaviors to humans if they are removed from their littermates and mother when they are two weeks old.

Oscar

Oscar's was a rare case, in which everything about him was known. His father was the next-door-neighbor's friendly black cat, his mother gave birth to her kittens in the Faber family's home, and the Fabers played with the kittens as soon as Mehitabel, the mother, would let them. So it came as no surprise to anyone that Oscar loved people. All his siblings did, too. When the Fabers' neighbors had guests who picnicked on the lawn, the kittens would march over and sit on the people's laps. And when the Fabers had guests, the kittens would sit on the guests' laps and feet.

That's how Oscar adopted his family. At 12 weeks of age, he sat on a visitor's feet, looked her in the eyes, and seemed to say, "Take me home." Oscar liked most people—especially children—dogs, and other cats, especially if they were orange tabbies like him. He was a result of friendly genes and human intervention during the critical developmental period.

Socialization, Problem Behaviors, and Normal Social Behavior

Mismatches Can Occur

Because we usually adopt cats who are well beyond their critical developmental periods, we have no input into the cat's early development and can only have a small influence on later development. Sometimes a cat owner and her feline companion can have different temperaments and the owner may expect the cat to engage in behaviors that the cat just does not do. You may adopt a cat hoping that it will be friendly and be good company for your child, but the cat may be aloof and may like only you.

For example, Sally was taken in at five months of age. She was a skinny kitten who appeared shy and possibly abused. The owners hoped she would be a companion to their young son. But it took years before Sally was anything other than a cat who just happened to live with the family. Today, she still doesn't like to be touched and easily hisses and spits. But she loves strangers and will run up to them to be petted—only unsheathing her claws after a satisfactory head rub (the vicious animal in cuddly cat clothing).

What do you do when you have a cat like Sally? Do you throw her out into the street, as many people would, send her to the animal shelter, or place a "cat available" sign up on lampposts?

Probably the best thing to do is to change how you behave toward the cat. Sally, for example, just isn't cuddly. Don't cuddle her. But if you were to allow Sally to come to you when she wants petting, rather than initiating the petting from your end, you may find that Sally enjoys an occasional head rub and may even come back for more. Eventually, she may feel so secure and confident with members of the family that she may even sit on their laps or sleep with them.

Bill is a very aggressive, 30-pound cat. He wants to play. He will knock down the family's Chihuahua with a hind limb kick, and then roll over the dog in a wrestling match. If the dog isn't available, he may try this sort of activity on your leg. But if his owners were to play with him more gently, and spend more time doing so, he may get the point and calm down a bit. If your play style is of the rough-and-tumble kind that leaves you riddled with scratches and bites, you might consider introducing gentler games, such as pulling a bathrobe tie along a floor for the cat to pounce on—instead of pouncing on your flesh.

Something to keep in mind, however, is that some traits in an adult are hard to change. Studies done on cats' socialization to people and cats' personalities and individualities confirm this element of steadfastness in a cat's personality. You should especially be aware of this when you are considering adopting an adult cat whose history is not known to you. And the older the cat, the less likely he will change his relationship toward people through learning. Your best bet, then, is to carefully consider the cat's personality at the time you are selecting one, and, once you have chosen one to adopt, learn to accept him as he is.

Four Critical Stages of Kitten Development

The developmental stages of a kitten's life comprise a continuous process. However, four periods within this span are of special importance: the infantile or neonatal period, which extends for the first 10 days of life; the transitional or intermediate period, which is from the 10th day to the 14th day; the socialization period, which extends from the 15th day of life through to the middle of the sixth week of life; and the adolescent or juvenile period, which begins in the early part of the fourth month.

The infantile/neonatal period

- This time is characterized by neonatal ingestive and sleep patterns. During this time, postural reflexes begin to develop and the cat is able to orient to a source of sound. Nursing is initiated by the queen, elimination is reflexive in response to maternal stimulation, and the kitten is sensitive to human handling, which may aid in its social orientation to humans.

The transitional/intermediate period

- Beginning during the second week of life when the eyelids open. This stage is marked by the appearance of some mobility and increased visual acuity.

The socialization period

- The single most important period during the cat's life—perhaps from two to seven weeks of age—is the time when the kitten begins to form social bonds with humans and other animals. Play behavior is first seen, and spontaneous elimination begins. Although the kitten is not weaned during this period, this is when the kitten begins to initiate feeding with help from his mother, rather than the queen initiating the feeding. Numerous gross motor skills that the kitten will need are developed at this time.

Adolescence

- A cat becomes an adolescent at about four months of age, when males learn how to mount and grip a female for copulation. In fact, a female's first estrus may be as early as the fourth month, although it is more likely to occur when the cat is five or six months old. During adolescence, not only are mating behaviors learned, but hunting behaviors also are perfected and play behavior decreases.

If you give a kitten a mouse . . .

- The socialization process isn't limited just to humans: Kittens exposed even to members of species considered to be their natural enemies (e.g., dogs, rats, mice, and birds) can develop bonds with them during this time. Thus, you can begin to appreciate the underpinnings of the kitten's early social environment when you encounter the not uncommon news photo of hamsters snuggled up against the family cat, for example. Once a cat is past the socialization phase, however, it is extremely difficult to condition the cat to tolerate or accept an individual of another species as a companion, especially if the species is more likely to be prey to cats.

Socialization, Problem Behaviors, and Normal Social Behavior

While socialization is critical in creating a friendly cat, keep in mind that your kitten's basic personality derives from its parents.

Problem Behaviors

Improper Socialization

Young kittens who have not had a chance to socialize will show problems as they get older. If they are removed from their littermates earlier than five weeks of age, they might not be able to socialize properly with other cats. Their interactions with humans may be marked by timidity, aggression, or an over-attachment. They may even resort to self-mutilation to gain attention. If the cat owner responds by giving the cat more attention, this may serve to reinforce the cat's extreme behavior. Their inability to identify with members of their species may cause them to be aggressive toward other cats or impair their ability to mate and raise their young. A kitten raised without her littermates and mother may not learn how to use her teeth and claws in appropriate ways, compromising her abilities to engage in normal feline behavior.

How to Handle "Isolated Syndrome"

If, by eight weeks of age, a cat has had little exposure to other species, he may become aggressive toward others. Known as "isolated syndrome," this behavior becomes more pronounced during times of stress to the cat, such as when the owner gives a party.

A cat who is unaccustomed to humans may learn to adjust to one or two persons in his life, but is quickly overwhelmed if besieged with more than that. Overcrowding—experienced as stress by the cat—can trigger aggression directed even toward those he accepts. A useful recourse in this case is to isolate the stressed-out cat in a room away from company and noise. If the problem is extreme, you may sedate the cat while handling her

---

Species Identification

The socialization period is also a time when kittens learn to relate to other cats—as well as to other species. Recognizing other cats sets the stage for later mating. It also allows cats to socialize with one another when necessary. A cat raised with members of the same species in addition to members of another species learns to accept both, but will form stronger bonds with the felines. If a cat is reared with a member of another species, she may later fail to respond to her own kind. Stress or emotional upset (e.g., hunger, pain, or loneliness) will hasten the socialization process and species identification.

a great deal in order to desensitize her.

A cat suffering from the isolated syndrome significantly limits the social environment the cat owner may create around the cat. Therefore, it is wise to choose a feline companion carefully: Avoid adopting an older cat or kitten of unknown background. If you are considering accepting the runt of a litter, be advised that it may have been intimidated by its littermates during its socialization period, curtailing its ability to socialize normally.

Fighting

Fighting is considered to be another "bad" feline behavior. To expect all cats to be friendly with fellow felines all the time is expecting more from them than we expect from ourselves. Cats, like humans, have their likes and dislikes. We have no way of predicting which cats will like one another and which will dislike each other. But if you put them in a room together and fireworks break out, you know there is a problem. Having fighting cats at home, however, is often as miserable for the owner as it is for the cats.

How to Stop Fighting Between Your House Cats

A couple married for only a few months recently had a vexing problem and turned to Cornell's Animal Behavior Clinic in search of a solution. The problem was their cats. One of the partners brought to the new home a very aggressive cat, possessive of his territory. The other partner brought two good-natured cats. The aggressive cat had learned not to be aggressive in the presence of his owners, but he

---

Kittenproofing Tips

- As your kitten becomes more comfortable, slowly increase the size of his domain.
- Make sure that litter boxes are easily accessible, located in quiet areas, and that the litter is changed regularly.
- Praise the kitten when she uses the litter box. By reinforcing good litter habits early, you'll avoid problems down the line.
- Kittenproof your home by removing fragile family heirlooms and anything else you'd hate to see broken.
- Be aware that a curious kitten can squeeze into the motor of a refrigerator or other appliance, or get stuck inside a reclining chair.
- Be careful with electrical cords and open windows, and put childproof locks on cabinets.
- To keep damage to curtains and upholstery to a minimum, trim your kitten's nails. Ask your veterinarian to show you how to do it, if you find it difficult—or you may choose to have it done for you by a professional.
- Provide your kitten with a kitty tree or condo for climbing.

Bringing Home a Kitten

Let us assume that you have picked a kitten who has been socialized to humans, and you want to bring her home. There are things you can do to start off on the right foot—or paw—with a kitten, beginning with the moment you take your new cat home.

You'll need an airline crate or carrier to transport your kitten. The crate can later serve as a safe haven when the kitty needs some soothing. Line it with an old towel or blanket; if possible, let your kitten's littermates and mother lie on the cloth to infuse it with their smells. Put a few pieces of dry kitten food in the crate to make it more enticing.

When you arrive home, first confine your new kitten to a small area—maybe a bedroom or bathroom. You want to acclimate him to your home slowly and not overwhelm him with strange new surroundings. If possible, surround him with as many familiar objects as possible—his old water bowl, toys, etc. Use the brand of food and litter that he's accustomed to and get a kitten-size litter box with sides low enough for easy entering and exiting. Keep the crate with its door propped open in the room, to allow him to use it as a cozy refuge.

If you have another cat, be sensitive to her needs as well. Your current cat will view the new one as an intruder. Don't upset the old-timer's routine by doing things such as putting the kitten's litter box where hers used to be. Keep their food and litter separate until they have grown accustomed to each other. Your current cat may hiss at the newcomer and even at you. This, too, will usually pass.

And to help turn your kitten into a well-adjusted cat, expose him early to all kinds of people (male, female, old, young) and all sorts of noises (the vacuum cleaner, radio, dishwasher). If the kitten flees to the farthest corner of the house and stays there for three hours when you vacuum near him, don't keep him near the vacuum cleaner the next time you turn it on.

Keep him busy

Put lots of toys in the room to keep him busy. A ping-pong ball or even a rolled-up piece of paper works well. Whatever your choice, make sure that it's big enough so that the kitten won't swallow it. Attach objects to string, then dangle them from doorknobs to keep your new arrival busy—but make sure the string is strong enough not to break or the kitten might swallow it.

Kittens can be veritable annoyance machines. Be ready for some stalking behavior. Cats are hunters. They sneak up on people's feet and pounce. To discourage this, clap your hands to scare the kitten, or spray him with water when he's ready to attack. Redirect the behavior onto an object by dragging a string or bathrobe tie along the floor or using a cat-fishing pole. To dampen the cat's nocturnal activities, play with him during the day and tire him out so he'll sleep at night. If you have to lock your kitten out of your room to get a good night's sleep, do not open the door when he meows, no matter how cute or pathetic he sounds. If you give in, you're in for a life with a manipulative feline.

—Fred Kent, DBVM

would escape from his room and go after the other cats when the couple was not home.

"Cats can wreck a marriage," says Katherine Houpt, VMD, PhD, director of the clinic. There is no way of knowing in advance whether newly introduced cats will get along, except that males tend to be more territorial and aggressive. In addition, behavior that perplexes the cat owner might be either fairly normal or a serious problem. Whatever the case, there are techniques to ameliorate the problem and bring about feline armistice, if not outright peace, to your household.

The following recommendations can be adapted for any new cat joining a household:

- Keep the new cat in one room so he can't interact with the resident cat or cats while he learns that he has a particular space in the house.

- The cats will nonetheless be making vocal and olfactory contact. You can speed up this process by rubbing each cat with the same towel, concentrating on the cheeks and the top of the tail, near its base, where glands are present.

- You also can exchange clean litter pans, which still carry the smell of the other cat. "If neither cat is hissing or growling or digging through [the walls] to the other, you can release them after a week or so and they will probably be okay," says Dr. Houpt. An additional caution for the new cat is to try to prevent his escape from the house until he has been in the house for a week or more. This will give him an opportunity to adjust and, one hopes, to feel secure in this new environment. If a new cat gets outside before he adjusts to the inside environment, he is less likely to return. Neither environment gives him a sense of security.

- Have the new cat neutered, since neutered animals tend to socialize better.

There are occasions when two cats who live happily together suddenly fight. Usually, says Dr. Houpt, the odor of one cat has changed as a result of visiting the veterinarian or a cat show, or taking a bath. "Smell is more important than vision," she says. Some changes can trigger a predatory response. "If you bring home a cat who is still groggy from the vet, it can trigger predatory aggression. Cats are not very nice in human ethical terms, but they are very good predators. They beat up on weaker cats."

Fear-Based Aggression

To counter fear-based aggression, in which a cat who is feeling threatened lashes out against the perceived aggressor, a good approach is to use a procedure that builds on the technique for introducing new cats. First, separate the cats in the house, then feed the aggressor—who probably is the one doing the chasing—only in a cat carrier. For about a week, put the carrier at one end of the room and the other cat's dish at the other end. Feed both in the same room. If neither cat growls or hisses, move the dishes closer to the carrier until the cats are feeding on either side of the carrier's door. The aggressor should still be separated. Then put the aggressor on a harness or leash to determine his attitude toward the scared cat. Move the dishes to opposite ends of the room. Move them closer only if there is no sign of aggression. Eventually, you can allow the aggressor loose with the victim for meals only. Otherwise, keep the cats separated until an aggression-free week has passed.

An additional step in severe cases is for the veterinarian to prescribe medications for both the

Hansel and Gretel

Hansel and Gretel, brother and sister littermates, about four years old, were available for adoption from a veterinarian's assistant. Both were strictly indoor cats and came feline leukemia virus (FELV)-tested (negative) with all their vaccinations up to date. The family members lost their hearts to Hansel—an orange tabby with white—and decided to take both.

Gretel hid behind a credenza for a week and refused to come out to eat or use the litter box. She would sneak out at night to use the floor as a litter box, then hide again. Hansel hid in a radiator, but was coaxed out by children and wanted to play. The original owner took Gretel back, where she did well as an only cat in her familiar home.

Hansel became less shy and played with the wife and children; he got along well with the family's other cats and dog. But he remained terrified of the husband. His terror of all adult males made it clear that he must have been punished or abused by a man. The family, however, was patient. It took four years before Hansel was willing to let the husband pet and hold him. He slowly became more trustful, no longer running and hiding when the husband moved toward him. Eventually, he would sleep on the husband's pillow, cuddling on his head. Once the bond of trust was established, Hansel was always affectionate. Many years later, when he died of an autoimmune disease, he was in the husband's arms.

aggressive and the fearful cat. Serious injury is rare in these housemate fights, but nevertheless, claws should be trimmed and blunt.

As a rule, breed and age are not important factors in assessing aggressive behavior. Certain medical conditions that come with aging, such as hyperthyroidism, are the exception and may cause aggressive behavior.

The owner should be aware of another, more widespread, condition of cat society. New kittens might be accepted into a household with other cats, and everyone involved is pleased. "But the newer cats are treated like adults when they become adults and they are expected to leave," says Dr. Houpt. "If they don't leave, the other cats may become very aggressive." What to do? Separate them, of course, and hope, with time, that they will at least grow to tolerate one another.

An Unaffectionate Cat

We all know someone who says she doesn't like cats because "they're unfriendly, too aloof, too independent." As a cat owner and lover, you probably take exception to this sort of statement. But what if your cat really seems to dislike you? She runs away from you, perhaps, or seems not to want to sit in your lap?

Some cats, like some people, are extremely shy. A genetic problem makes them likely to be victimized and afraid. If you have two cats and one seems to be afraid, she may be intimidated by your other cat—and possibly by you. She is most likely to be afraid of people she does not know. This also can be a problem related to inadequate socialization.

If you suspect that your cat is fearful, try not to impose yourself on her. Always let her come to you, and be sure that when you do pet her, you do it gently and avoid patting her on the head. Induce her to play with you by using interactive toys, such as the "fishing pole" that dangles a piece of cloth. Even using your shoelaces or bathrobe sash will suffice. Try entertaining her in the evening, as most cats like to play then. Also, try to get her to interact with you when you feed her meals or treats. But before you decide the problem is with the kitty, ask yourself if you may be to blame. It could be something subtle, like your perfume or cologne, that irritates her, or, if you wear silky, slippery clothes that don't allow her to hold on when she sits in your lap. If you jump up every other minute, or if you stroke her fur the wrong way, it may irk her. Cats with long hair may become too warm when they sit on your lap. Not all cats are equally friendly, but if you use the correct approach, most can be good companions.

Aggression to Humans

What about the cat who attacks your feet whenever you walk by, or bites you when you try to pet her? The cat suffers from feline aggression, a common complaint among cat owners. Feline aggression can be divided into three basic types:

1. Fear-induced aggression. This occurs whenever the cat is frightened, such as a visit to a veterinarian or a move to a new home.

2. Redirected aggression. This can occur when the cat is annoyed by something else—let's say he is fighting with another cat. If you intervene, you may suffer from your cat's ire. When Miss Kitty is being stalked by her archenemy, and you pick her up to cuddle, she may turn on you.

3. Play aggression. This is really the equivalent of a feline amusement ride. The cat is stalking something, in typical feline hunting fashion. The only problem is that the something he is stalking is your foot.

Cats may also become aggressive because of sexual stimulation. If they find stroking sexually stimulating, they may first knead you with their paws, then drool on you, and last, bite. If this happens, stop petting your cat immediately and refrain from petting him in like fashion or duration in the future.

Preventing Aggression When Introducing New Cats

If you are bringing a new cat into a household that already has one or more cats, you will need to introduce her gradually in order for the cats to accept one another. As we have noted earlier, you may also need to perform the same introductory process for a cat who has been sick or hospitalized, for she will smell different to the other resident cats, and this may trigger aggression.

This is the same basic method used to prevent cats in the same household from fighting.

The olfactory adjustment stage

Place the cats in separate parts of the house to allow them to get accustomed to each other's smells. Place the new cat in a separate room with food, water, and litter for a few days so that the resident cat or cats become familiar with the new cat's odors and sounds. Cornell's Dr. Houpt also recommends increasing olfactory contact between the cats during this olfactory adjustment period by rubbing both cats' cheeks with the same towel daily and exchanging their litter boxes. Make sure their boxes are kept clean and that both cats are free of infectious organisms that can be passed in their feces.

The adjustment period varies and depends on the age of the resident cat: The older the cat, the less able he is to acclimate to a newcomer.

In the second stage, put the cats into separate cat carriers to protect the new cat while the two cats get used to seeing each other in the same room. Lastly, open the carrier to allow the new cat to come and go at will to complete the acclimatization process.

You also can leave the cats in adjoining rooms and partially open the door between them. This allows them to venture toward one another at their own initiative. Another option is to insert a screen door between the two cats' rooms. "The owner can

Respond Quickly to Aggression

Don't ignore aggressive behavior. React instantly: Keep a spray bottle filled with water on hand to "spritz" your cat each time he attacks. You also can try spraying an animal repellent or even rubbing an antiperspirant on your pants legs. Antiperspirants contain alum, a drying ingredient that will parch a cat's tongue and paws to discourage attacks. Speaking loudly or shaking an empty soda can that is partially filled with coins are also good, low-tech cat deterrents.

The Long-Term Approach

- Your cat may be aggressive because he has excess energy. Give him some exercise at least twice a day for 10-minute periods. Throw some balls for him to bat around or retrieve, get him some catnip toys, roll up some aluminum foil balls, or play with him with a cord or bathrobe sash.
- Get him a new scratching post or a cat condominium—carpeted boxes on piles that serve as cat playgrounds.
- Let him look out the window and watch the birds or, if he happens to like the TV, buy him a cat entertainment video (videos of birds, fish, and squirrels).

also encourage them to play together by sliding a feather toy under the door separating them, allowing them to play with the same toy and, we hope, each other," suggests Dr. Houpt. Food can also be used to shape the cats' behavior, especially when they are hungry. Feed them at the same time on the opposite sides of the door to reward them in one another's presence by the food.

When the cats begin to play together and groom one another, you will have succeeded in introducing the new cat into the household.

Overcrowding

If yours is a multicat household, don't be surprised if some of the resident cats who have accepted newcomers in the past begin to behave strangely when faced with yet one more feline. Your cats are sending you the message that overcrowding is occurring. However, if you familiarize the cats with one another as outlined previously, the behavioral changes should diminish. If they do not, you can isolate the cats responsible in small groups, and then gradually allow them access again to the rest of the house. A useful technique to cut down on stress in houses with cat colonies is to arrange shelves or boxes for each animal. This affords individuals some privacy and the chance to claim some space of their own.

You may need to spend more time alone with one or more of your cats, grooming them or permitting them to sleep on your lap. The extra care or extra stroking has helped some cats who sense competition from other cats in the household. Another solution is to reduce the number of cats in the home by finding a new home for one or more of them, or opening other parts of the house to some of them.

Normal Social Behaviors

Indications of a Cat's Friendliness

When a cat enters a social group, she will display signs of friendliness by purring, rubbing, and raising her tail. The raised tail provides a visual signal that the cat is relaxed and friendly. The signals are part of the cat's normal routine and serve to maintain stable social relationships with other cats in the animal's life. Blinking also indicates friendliness, whereas a prolonged stare is used to intimidate. A subordinate cat may react to the stare by withdrawing. A cat who is not aggressive will blink when staring at other cats, signaling that the scrutiny is not hostile.

Cats who are companions to humans also display these same friendly behaviors. However, because the human-cat relationship is less competitive than an interspecific relationship, the meaning of some of these signals may evolve into something different. For example, the cat initially rubs the human to mark the owner with the cat's scent. But if the owner reinforces the behavior by stroking the cat, the cat will rub to seek attention.

Body Language and Other Signs

Within the first few days of a kitten's life, she imprints on her mother based on smell. The infant-maternal relationship has a lasting effect on the cat's behavior. For example, if your cat comes up to you and purrs, or kneads while in your arms, or lies down to be petted, she is demonstrating this holdover from her infancy. Humans may even have selectively bred cats for these pleasing behaviors. Also, when your cat approaches you with her tail held high, she is greeting you. Licking you communicates a different message: She is grooming you as she would a kitten or a friendly adult cat. If a male licks you, he may be courting you.

Why do cats purr?

Domestic cats resemble many other species of cat in their ability to purr, although it is often claimed that the large roaring cats (genus *Panthera*, such as the lion, *Panthera leo*) do not do it. According to veterinary behaviorist Bonnie V. Beaver, DVM, in her text, *Feline Behavior: A Guide for Veterinarians* (Philadelphia, Pennsylvania: W.B. Saunders Co., 1992), purring results from movement of some of the muscles of the larynx with the glottis partially closed. The purr can be produced with the mouth closed and can be continued for long periods.

Purring almost certainly is a form of communication inasmuch as it indicates to others that the purring animal is in a particular state (presumably relaxed and contented). Kittens first purr while suckling when they are a few days old. Their purring may signal to the mother that all is well, much like the smile of a baby. In effect, the purr may help to establish and maintain a close relationship.

Probably, for similar reasons, the purr is used by adult cats in social and sexual contexts. For instance, an adult female will purr while suckling her kittens and when she courts a male. Again, like the human smile, purring can be used by a subordinate animal to appease a dominant one. The implication is that purring reduces the likelihood of attack. Whether or not relationships are impaired when purring does not occur has not been investigated.

Why do cats rub?

Rubbing parts of their bodies against objects and other animals is a common feline behavior. The reasons underlying this behavior may include friendliness when the cat is relaxed, scent-marking, and conferring a dominant status to another cat in the group. Relaxed and friendly rubbing occurs toward humans as well as among feral cats in a group.

Certain areas of the cat's body—between the ears and eyes, the lips, the chin, and the tail—contain glands that produce secretions. The cat makes use of these glands to scent-mark, using different parts for different targets. Thus, he tends to use his lips, chin, and tail to mark objects and his head patches and tail to mark other cats. Marking with the head patch may allow for all of the cats in a social group to have a similar smell. This common odor may help to show kinship among the group.

Early in the courting process, the male, who typically comes from outside the female's social group, and the female will engage in head rubbing. Lip rubbing also carries some significance: In studies, a wooden peg that had been lip-rubbed by a female cat was sniffed longer by male cats than was an unmarked peg. How long the males sniff most likely depends on the female's estrous state. In the early stages of estrus, the female will frequently rub with her tail, signaling to passing males that she is in heat.

Cats will also rub objects and humans with their tail or upper lips and chin in a nonsexual context. Cats often will rub their lips along the corners of new cardboard boxes, or on head-height branches and twigs on plants. This behavior is especially pronounced after a confident cat has had an aggressive encounter with another animal. In the absence of other cats, a cat may rub her tail, chin, and upper lip on items to announce her presence. Here, rubbing may serve a similar function as spraying.

Differences among cats

While domestic cats may belong to a single species, as individuals they may have distinctly different— even singular—personalities. An active area of research focuses on how the early environment of a kitten helps to shape these individual traits. Currently, we have more knowledge on how genes influence the morphological (structural) characters of the cat, such as coat color and length; what is missing is a better understanding of how genetic influences help to determine a cat's individual behaviors. Along with genetic factors, the interplay between the cat's behavior and the caregiver's behavior helps to determine the personality of a cat.

Chapter 2

Grooming: Normal and Destructive

Normal Grooming

People like cats because they are so clean—they groom. And grooming is a very serious ritual. Grooming behaviors are carried out in very stereotyped manners. Stereotyped behaviors are repeated and done in the same manner by most or all members of the same species. They tend to be influenced by genetics. And although these behaviors serve to keep the cat clean, they may result in fur all over your velvet cushions, favorite black slacks, or other areas where the cat likes to sit and preen. And they also may result in hairballs that the cat will vomit up, leaving you presents on your Oriental rugs and expensive upholstery.

Licking the Nose and Lips

For example, licking the nose and lips constitutes a simple form of grooming. After she eats or drinks, your cat will run her tongue along the edge of the upper lips to the corners of her mouth.

Face Washing

Face washing is yet another form of grooming. Feline face washing is a stereotyped behavior, meaning that the actions carried out are precisely orchestrated and genetically determined. All cats do pretty much the same thing in the same order. During face washing, the cat will use her front paw to transfer saliva from her mouth to her face. She will rub her paw in a circular motion that gets wider with each new round. Then she will apply her paw down the backside of her ears, and over her forehead and eye.

Other Areas

When she grooms other areas of her body, the cat's actions are not stereotyped. Typically, she will run her tongue over her fur using long strokes applied in the same direction that her fur grows. Depending on which region of her body she is grooming, the cat will either lie down or sit to do this. The saliva that she applies during grooming is typically licked up again. However, in a hot environment, the saliva remains on her fur to help cool her body by evaporation.

It is important for an owner to try to help the cat stay groomed by combing or brushing her coat on a regular basis. This will cut down on the cat hairs around the house and reduce the fur balls that can accumulate in her stomach.

Hairballs

When your cat does regurgitate or vomit up a hairball, don't punish her. It's something she can't help doing. But make sure you have cleaning materials around so that you can clean it up without leaving a stain on carpeting, upholstery, or other fabrics or surfaces.

To prevent hairballs, you may want to dose your cat with one of the many very palatable hairball removal and prevention remedies, such as Petromalt® or Laxatone®. And remember to brush her regularly so she has fewer hairballs.

When Good Grooming Affects Your Furniture

Clawing and scratching are behaviors that come naturally to cats. They do this partly for social reasons—for example, to mark, to threaten, to display behavior in the presence of other cats, during play, during bouts of estrous rolling, as an expression of excitement around humans, or to scent-mark by smearing secretions from their feet onto scratching posts. And this partly conditions their claws. Clawing leaves a visible pattern in the area clawed, and it also leaves the scent of paw sweat, both important feline marking activities.

Scratching also serves an hygienic role: Cats remove their outer, frayed claw, allowing a new, sharper claw growing underneath to become exposed. Normally, a tree or other wooden surface would be the object used for the cat to sharpen her claws. For the housebound cat, however, the only suitable objects on which to exercise her scratching tendencies may be your furniture. You may notice that your cat will choose prominent scratching targets and areas in the home; these items take on significance with repeated scratching, resulting in further marking.

Start Training Early

Good scratching habits can be encouraged while your cat is still a kitten. Training your cat to use a scratching post early on will help protect the furniture. The following tips on choosing and installing the post should help:

- Height—Choose a stable post approximately 2.5–3–feet high, to allow the cat to stand on his hind feet and reach out to claw.

- Texture—The fabric should have a longitudinal weave and be made of loosely woven material or sisal. A tight weave will not allow the cat to work her claws into the fabric. Other options are carpet-covered, floor-to-ceiling cat trees, real bark-covered logs, or catnip-impregnated corrugated cardboard.

- Placement—The post should be the most prominent vertical surface in the area, as this satisfies the cat's scratching proclivities. Because cats scratch and stretch more often when they awaken, one post should be placed near the cat's usual sleeping place. Another post should be placed in a prominent spot where the cat will use it. Some cats prefer horizontal scratching surfaces. They should be accommodated or your rugs will suffer.

- Encouragement—You can encourage your kitten to use the post by placing a favorite toy on top, by sprinkling it with catnip to make it enticing, by leaving the kitten in a room where the post is the only furniture, or by having an older, post-trained cat nearby to teach the kitten by example. The best teacher of a kitten is her mother, so, if possible, kittens should be obtained from queens who use a scratching post. (Or you can try to teach your cat to use one by example!)
- Adopt a kitten whose mother uses a scratching post. You may want to wait until the kitten is 12 weeks old to take him home, so you will be sure he has learned to use the post.
- Once the kitten has started using the post, it will become a favorite scratching object if you keep the original post where it is and do not replace it until it is so shredded that replacement becomes a necessity. And, once the cat becomes used to using it, never move it!

What to Do About Furniture Clawing

Do not punish your cat for scratching, as this will only make him run from you. If you discourage scratching but do not provide an acceptable substitute for the furniture, the cat's scratching threshold may decrease, spurring more frequent and unsuccessful attempts to scratch—and making him increasingly frustrated.

Behavioral modification

If your furniture continues to take a beating from your cat, you may wish to use behavioral modification to retrain him. First, remove the targeted furniture (or move and cover it with plastic) and replace it with a scratching post. If the carpet is the target, position the scratching post over the commonly clawed area. Next, when you spot the cat scratching areas other than the post, admonish him by startling him with a clap. Later, entice him to the post and encourage him to scratch it.

An indirect form of discipline that does not connect the aversive tactic to you is to use a remotely controlled, water-filled plant sprayer, and spray the cat when he claws your valuable furniture. A cat owner can also attempt to use smell aversion, using olfactory cues. With this tactic, the owner sprays a scented mist at a 90-degree angle from the cat's face, while making a threatening gesture toward the cat's face with the can. This sequence makes the cat fearful of the odor associated with that event. Next, with the cat out of the room, spray the scratched object well with the scented material and allow the mist to settle before the cat returns to the area. You must still provide a suitable replacement for the cat to scratch.

When you must leave the cat alone, he should be in a room where scratching has not been a problem. You can also minimize the damage your cat causes when scratching by clipping her claws: Less damage is done if claws are short. Another unique method to protect your furniture is to use a product called Soft Paws® nail caps. These are soft caps that come in several colors and sizes that you glue onto your cat's claws. They cover the point of the nail so the nail can no longer catch in upholstery and other fabrics. They need to be replaced every few weeks. They cost $14.95 a set, plus $2.50, shipping and handling by mail. Soft Paws are available on the Web at www.softpaws.com or from your veterinarian.

The Question of Declawing

If all else fails, the cat should be declawed rather than euthanized or sent to a shelter. For many cat owners, surgical declawing is unacceptable. Thus, some veterinary surgeons are now using a procedure called tenectomy, removing a section of the tendon controlling the muscle in the forepaw that allows claws to project. The theory behind this is that tenectomy is a less traumatic surgery than declawing, which involves removing the claw and part of the bone of the toe.

In an article written by Arthur J. Jankowski, VMD, and colleagues from the University of Pennsylvania School of Veterinary Medicine, published in the August 1, 1998, issue of the *Journal of the American Veterinary Association,* the researchers compared cats who underwent tenectomy with those who underwent the more radical declawing procedure, called onychectomy. They evaluated the cats based on the amount of pain the cats appeared to be suffering within the first day after the surgery, the types and numbers of complications the cats were reported as having in the immediate postsurgical period, the length of time it took for the cats to walk normally after surgery, and owner satisfaction with the procedure.

As expected, the researchers found that cats undergoing tenectomy appeared to be in less pain postsurgically than those who had their claws removed. The numbers of complications shortly after the surgery—hemorrhage, infection, lameness, and behavioral changes—were about the same in both groups. But, unexpectedly, owners appeared to be less satisfied with the results of the tendon removal than they were with total declawing. The reason was that cats still had claws and more than half the cats still could scratch. Furthermore, after tenectomy, the claws grow thicker than do normal, movable claws that can be kept trim through scratching. Therefore, it was difficult to cut the cats' claws.

The clinicians warn that owners who choose tenectomy should be aware that the cats still have their foreclaws after surgery, and the claws may need frequent trimming. Also, the thick claws are esthetically unpleasing.

Cornell's Dr. James R. Richards points out that people whose cats don't allow them to trim their claws should not consider tenectomy for their cat. He remarks that a cat who won't allow his claws to be trimmed before surgery certainly will not allow them to be trimmed after surgery.

Some people are adamantly opposed to declawing as inhumane. But if declawing a cat keeps the cat in a home rather than being thrown out in the street or placed in a shelter where euthanasia is possible, it saves a cat's life.

Chapter 3

Housesoiling

Cat owners' most frequent complaint about their cat's behavior is that the cat is housesoiling—urinating or defecating in areas outside of the litter box. This behavioral problem is the one most likely to cause a cat owner to seek professional behavioral counseling for the animal. By some estimates, about 10 percent of house cats have an inappropriate elimination problem at some time in their lives; but, in fact, the actual numbers may be much higher.

The reasons for such behavior may be numerous. A cat may suffer from a urinary tract disorder or from disease of the large intestine. Stresses in the home, especially when there are other cats in the household, may make the litter box an insecure place for a cat. In still other cases, the problem may be as simple as the cat not liking the texture or odor of the litter.

No matter the cause, it is your job as the owner to work with your veterinarian to try to determine why this behavior is occurring, and to make the litter box a place your cat wants to visit at the appropriate times.

Eliminative Behavior Development

Unlike human newborns, who urinate and defecate at will, newborn kittens need mechanical stimulation of the anogenital area in order to eliminate. This is called the urogenital reflex. The mother cat will lick or stroke with her tongue the kitten's anogenital region and the kitten will urinate or defecate. The mother then ingests the kitten's waste products. This kind of behavior probably developed in the cat's wild ancestors, who needed to keep their nests clean so there would not be an odor to attract predators to the nest containing the young. By the time a kitten is 21 days old, it can eliminate on its own without its mother's stimulation, and the reflex disappears entirely when the kitten is between 23 and 39 days old.

In modern-day house cats, this reflex serves to make cats, as they get older, maintain the desire to remain clean—both in their body and in their environments. This reflexive behavior works well for us, the owners, because, with few exceptions, it gives us a very clean house pet. But it also means that the cats have expectations of us: We are expected to keep their litter boxes clean, something not all of us remember to do as often as we should. And when cats' misbehavior manifests itself as an "out-of-litter-box experience," the first question we should ask ourselves is, "Are we cleaning the litter box often enough?"

What Cats Do

In a recent survey, about a quarter of cat owners reported that their cats did not use the litter box. Of 62 behavioral cases recently presented to the Cornell University College of Veterinary Medicine's Small Animal Clinic, 41 involved spraying or inappropriate urination. While the sexes were almost equally represented (23 males and 18 females), there were distinct differences in how the two genders manifested their elimination problems. Males, for example, are more likely to spray than females. Under normal circumstances, cats are fastidiously clean in matters concerning their hygiene; therefore, some underlying cause for elimination misbehavior must exist.

Diagnosis

Treating your cat's problem requires that you first correctly track down its source. Elimination problems have different causes—hence different treatments—so it is important to identify which type is occurring. The problem must be narrowed to inappropriate defecation versus urination, and—if urination—spraying, which is a marking behavior, versus squatting, which may be a marking behavior, but usually results from a physical disorder. It is rare for a cat to exhibit both inappropriate defecation and urination.

Spraying or Squatting?

To differentiate between spraying and squatting, watch your cat's behavior and posture when he urinates. A cat who sprays will back up to an object situated approximately nose-high to him, extend his pelvic limbs, raise his tail, and spray a forceful, steady stream of urine. Alternatively, a cat will squat, which is the normal posture for urinating.

What if you are unable to catch your cat in the act? Even if the owner cannot directly observe the cat, it is possible to deduce which behavior is occurring based on the trail of evidence left behind.

Notice if the urine was aimed at vertical objects, such as a wall or curtains, or if it was directed at an individual's personal effects, such as a pillow, laundry, or favorite chair. If urine is detected in any of these vertical areas, then spraying is most likely the problem. In spraying, the cat releases only small volumes of urine, which is frequently directed at vertical objects. The objects targeted for spraying tend to have some form of social significance. For example, common targets are windows or doors, which afford the cat a view of other cats; beds and chairs, which can be associated with specific household members; or microwave ovens and stereo speakers, whose sounds may provoke the spraying.

Isolating just where a transgression takes place gives a better idea of where the problem may lie—and how to fix it. For example, the cat may be soiling only one room in the house. In this case, simply making that room off-limits to the cat may solve the problem. Unfortunately, sometimes the cat just finds another place to soil.

Large volumes of urine—left on rugs, along the edges of a room, or pooled in sinks or bathtubs—signify squatting. Beds, especially waterbeds or those lying directly on the floor, are also frequent targets of the squatting cat. Squatting urination in the wrong place usually indicates a desire for a clean litter box, a urinary tract disorder, or it may be related to social interactions between cats in the household. For example, one cat may keep another from the litter box.

Number One Problem

Topping the list of complaints about elimination—accounting for nearly half of all owner complaints about inappropriate elimination—is urinating outside the box. Inappropriate defecation problems account for 24–29 percent of complaints. The cat owner's observations, together with a veterinarian's careful history-taking, will help to assess the type of elimination causing the problem, how long the problem has existed, where the soiling is taking place, and how diligently the owner is maintaining a clean kitty box.

An important point to convey to your veterinarian is whether the cat has ever been litter-trained. If the cat has never been taught to use a box, then he is not doing anything that is inappropriate for him. However, if he has been so trained, then the investigation must focus on why the cat is behaving differently now. Another important clue is how long the problem has been occurring. If Kitty missed the litter box on only one occasion, she is not likely to require remediation. However, an ongoing, years-long history of not using the box poses a much more difficult challenge.

Scent-Marking

The urine of felines, like that of many mammals, is

Who Is the Culprit?

In a multicat household facing a problem with inappropriate urination, a key element to the puzzle is just which cat is responsible. An owner may mistakenly identify one cat just because she "looks guilty" or has never been a favorite. However, this type of singling out is not likely to resolve the problem: Treating the wrong cat does not address the real source of the problem and affords the owner no relief. One way to address this situation is to isolate your cats from one another until you can identify the culprit. If cats are separated, then it may result in no inappropriate elimination by any of the cats. That indicates that the problem is the social interactions among the cats.

Another technique allows you to identify the urine using fluorescein, a nontoxic dye that is available through your veterinarian. This fluorescent compound is excreted in the cat's urine. You give it orally to one cat at a time (starting with the most likely offender), then you check fresh urine spots with an ultraviolet light to detect the marked urine. Although all cat urine is fluorescent under black light, the addition of fluorescein makes it much brighter. If the cat in question is absolved, administer the compound to the next most likely cat. Staggering the administration of the dye to a different cat every two days should eventually lead you to the offender.

not simply a waste product to be expelled from the body; it is also replete with pheromones, compounds that contain odiferous molecules, which convey messages to other cats who sniff them. Unneutered males in particular use this olfactory means of communication, known as scent-marking. Most likely, the ingredient causing the tomcat urine's potent and (to humans) objectionable smell is a sulfur-containing amino acid called felinine, which may play an important role in passing along information in territorial spraying.

Spraying has the advantage of covering a wide area at the appropriate height for sniffing. Thus, male animals invest a good deal of time and energy marking sites within their home ranges—especially targets near borders, crossings, and pathways. (A home range is an area a cat regularly traverses.)

Once the cat chooses a site for marking, he sprays urine. Typically, the cat backs up to an object situated at about nose level and stands when he sprays, tail held erect and twitching erratically. Or, he may position himself front-end down, rear-end up, which may afford him a higher stream of spray. With either stance, his penis is directed toward his tail, which he characteristically wriggles.

Whether the stereotypic behavior of spraying is spurred by his neurological circuitry that is innate, or is voluntary, elicited by the visual cue of a vertical object, the purpose is achieved: The cat has marked his territory with his own, highly individualized scent. He may also mark other spots by cheek-rubbing.

Intact Male Behavior Problems

While you may notice, to your chagrin, that your unneutered male is behaving, well, like a tomcat, his behavior—which from your standpoint is perhaps objectionable—is normal for an intact male feline. The tomcat sprays his pungent-smelling urine mainly to mark his territory, particularly during mating season. Males' sprayed urine attracts estrous females (those in heat) to meet him during the mating season. You may want to think of this as male cat cologne or after-shave.

Your tomcat will be especially vigilant in his marking behavior if other tomcats pass through the area. Other drawbacks to the owner during the mating season are the house cat's increased activity and tendency to leave home, making him difficult to live with, as well as his increased risk of injuries and infections from dangerous microorganisms (such as the feline immunodeficiency virus or the feline leukemia virus) from fighting with other males. As for the mating behavior itself, the cat owner who finds himself an unwitting interloper may not appreciate its noisiness, especially if it unfolds under a bedroom window at night.

Castration is a good idea. It removes not only the ability to make sperm cells, so the cat is infertile, it also removes the major source of the hormone, testosterone, that stimulates the cat to spray, to fight, and to court females.

Why They Do It—Spraying

Normal Cat Behavior

To the surprise of many cat owners, urine spraying is a normal cat behavior. Cats who are targets of aggression tend to engage in spraying, and males and females typically mark trees, fence poles, shrubs, or walls along the routes they frequent. While as a rule, males tend to scent-mark (spray urine) more than females, both genders engage in the behavior, generally at predictable times of the day.

If the cat is subjected to a stressful situation or emotional disturbance, he or she will spray in response. When Miss Kitty notices her archenemy, Ralph, sitting on the sofa, she sprays the entire bottom of that piece

---

Anal Sacs House Pheromones

Anal sacs are a pair of glands located on either side of the anal opening. Scientists believe that the dark material they hold contains pheromones, chemicals animals use to communicate their gender, reproductive status, and presence in or "ownership" of a particular location to other members of their species. The odor of these chemicals also serves the same purpose when two strange cats meet face-to-face. At this juncture, they will circle one another in a ritual, positioning themselves to sniff in the perianal area, the area around the anus where fecal and anal sac odors most likely communicate the information they seek. This also helps to explain why cats, renowned for their fastidious nature, sometimes leave their feces uncovered when they are outside of their primary living area—the feces' odor most likely communicates information to other cats.

of furniture. Ralph, in turn, will spray the bottom of the sofa later that day. And the process will continue. Miss Kitty wins nothing by this, as Ralph won't give up the sofa. Ralph, meanwhile, thinks he's advertising to everyone that the sofa is his. The real losers are the owners who spend a fortune buying odor removers and upholstery cleaners to get rid of the smell and the discoloration.

Just how often the cat sprays depends on the individual cat, its gender, and its social status among other cats. Unneutered cats tend to spray more often during the breeding season. For example, free-ranging tomcats tend to spray a dozen times per hour, compared to once an hour for queens, or females—who especially spray when they are in heat.

The desire to eliminate scent-marking is one of the major reasons owners have their cats spayed or neutered. Despite this surgical removal of the sources of sex hormones, one out of 10 castrated males and one out of 20 spayed females will spray at least occasionally, as Ralph's and Miss Kitty's behaviors clearly attest.

Why do cats engage in scent-marking? Researchers believe that one function of spraying may be to help arrange temporary activities with other felines—among these activities is mating. Cats are able to tell the difference between the urine of familiar cats and that of strange cats. However, the message that urine conveys to other cats is short-lived—lasting only up to 24 hours. After this time, cats appear to lose interest in the marking. The sprayer must respray the area.

Scent-marking is communication. Remember that cats tend to be loners. They are not overly social animals and they do not tend to live in groups. Thus, how do cats in the wild manage to get together for important functions, such as mating, yet remain apart so that they don't fight? Scent-marking is a perfectly safe way to allow cats to leave a molecular trace or imprint of their presence, even after they have left an area. Other cats who then venture into the area shortly after the area was marked can pick up messages encoded in the urine that can influence their activities. By sniffing the urine, a cat can decipher the marker's gender, how long the marker remained in the area, and her reproductive status—all without having to actually encounter the cat and risk a possible skirmish. Thus, this method of communication allows cats to avoid surprise encounters and maximize their opportunities for overlap during receptive stages of their reproductive cycles.

Making a home his own

Cats will spray in order to acclimate to an area—usually when a tomcat is placed in new surroundings. In this case, the familiar smell of his own scent helps to reduce his anxiety over his new surroundings and reduce his aggression. Laying down his scent as a newcomer to the area also enables him to set up his own small breeding territory. If another cat of the same sex intrudes upon a resident cat's territory, the resident cat will increase his frequency of spraying.

One aspect that is not involved in urine spraying is competition. A cat sprays with the intent to provide her own scent. Similarly, a cat who smells another cat's urine does not find the pheromonal messages inherent in it to be either fearful or intimidating. And, unlike dogs, who urinate where another dog has marked, the cat is not provoked to cover the marking with her own urine—although the odor of feline urine, even a very old odor, tells the cat that this is a good place to urinate, too.

The more cats, the greater the likelihood of spraying

For castrated males or neutered females, the most common trigger for spraying is the whiff—hence evidence—of other cats in their surroundings. This is why a multicat household is more likely to be the scene of this problem than a single-cat household. There are also gender influences: Male cats who share quarters with a female are more likely to spray than males who live with another male. The

---

An Advertisement—Not a Threat

Does spraying urine on an object scare away intruders? For a cat, probably not. Urine-marking in cats may be an advertisement: "Hi, I'm an adult female in estrus, and I was here," or, "Hello, ladies! I'm a mature male looking for a quick tumble." It may also serve to keep other potential urine-markers away from the spot by advertising that an adult male has already been here—and he may be back. Behavioral researchers note that spraying indicates the cat is self-confident, so perhaps wimpy cats sniff but don't spray. (Frustrated cats also spray.)

situation gets worse as the number of cats living within a single household increases. Thus, homes with three, four, or more cats are almost guaranteed to encounter problems with spraying. According to some studies, the incidence of spraying jumped from 25 percent in single-cat households to 100 percent in households with more than 10 cats. Interestingly, once there are more than 18 cats in a household, spraying and aggression cease or are greatly reduced.

Other disturbances

A shift in the cat's normal routine, such as introducing a new cat to the home or moving into a new house, may precipitate spraying (see page 8). Once the animal becomes used to the change in circumstances, the spraying may subside. If the cat perceives a decrease in the amount of food he receives, is punished, or is exposed to overcrowding, he may spray. Another influencing factor is the time of year: Spraying tends to occur more in early spring and late summer.

Why They Do It—Inappropriate Urination and Defecation

Urinary Tract Problems

Feline lower urinary tract disease

A significant number of housesoiling cases are caused by cystitis (inflammation of the bladder), urethritis (inflammation of the urethra), or urethral blockage, which are associated with feline lower urinary tract disease (FLUTD). Your cat may develop FLUTD spontaneously and for unknown reasons. For general purposes, FLUTD may be divided into two broad areas: those cases in which there is precipitation of stones or granules composed of minerals, and those cases that do not involve stones or granules.

Mineral deposits in the urinary tract may cause irritation or urinary tract blockages. The two most common kinds of deposits are those made of struvite or those made of calcium oxalate. Struvite is the most common constituent of such deposits, but those containing calcium oxalate are increasing in frequency.

In some cases, a diet that is specifically formulated to prevent buildup of such deposits, especially a diet low in magnesium, producing acidic urine, may decrease production of struvite. Currently, most standard cat foods are formulated to these specifications, although some are particularly advertised as special diets for animals with urinary tract problems. Reduced calcium diets that don't promote formation of acidic urine are often suggested for cats who produce calcium oxalate deposits.

If your cat is urinating in inappropriate places and passing bloody urine, he or she is likely to be suffering from some form of urinary tract disease. Because urination may be painful or difficult, the cat begins to associate the litter box with the pain, and so voids outside the box. The cat may also suffer from urgency and be unable to make it to the box. Sometimes, when urination is uncomfortable for the cat because of lower urinary tract disease, the cat may wait until the last minute to use the litter box—and he may not make it. This may explain why you may find urine in the sink, the bathtub, and even on top of anything plastic. Affected cats seem to like urinating on plastic bags, upholstery covers, and similar surfaces.

Any inappropriate urination for which a behavioral cause cannot be determined requires an immediate veterinary visit. Any cat exhibiting straining, excessive licking of the genitalia, or hematuria (blood in the urine) should see the veterinarian immediately.

If you see your male cat straining to urinate and sitting up on his haunches like a bear, licking his penis, it may be because he is suffering from urethral obstruction. This, too, requires an immediate visit to the doctor.

Bear in mind that straining due to lower urinary tract disease is nothing to trifle with or experiment on. It may be a feline medical emergency and require immediate veterinary attention. A cat who may be straining at his litter box on Saturday, may end up comatose by Monday without proper and immediate veterinary intervention.

Problems With Defecation

Constipation

Many cats, especially as they age, are vulnerable to developing constipation. The constipated cat's experience of painful defecation may prompt her to choose a different site for elimination in an attempt to avoid the pain associated with using the litter box. Cats suffering from disorders of the large intestine or rectum may behave similar. Typical locations for inappropriate defecation are just outside the litter box, on rugs, in fireplaces, or in the soil of houseplants. Bear in mind that cats are not nuclear physicists. They cannot reason that if it hurts them to defecate, the problem is with them and not with the location of their litter box. They seem to think that if they defecate somewhere else, the pain will go away. We, of course, know otherwise. But how do we know if painful defecation is the reason for your feline's fecal mishaps?

First, discuss this with your veterinarian. After taking a complete medical history and doing a thorough physical examination, he or she may perform some selected diagnostic tests. If constipation is deemed to be the problem, he or she may advise you to change the cat's diet or to add a stool softener to the cat's food. It may be helpful if the cat relearns to use the litter box. Place another litter box at the site where the cat is now defecating. Once she starts using that box, you can slowly move it until it is in a more appropriate location. (Who wants a litter box in the middle of the living room floor?) Also, look at your cat's anal sacs. They can become impacted and/or infected, which can cause pain at defecation and lead to defecation in inappropriate areas. Ask your veterinarian if the anal sacs appear to be okay. If not, he or she can treat the problem accordingly.

Age-related changes

Changes in elimination behaviors may be age-related. For example, a very old cat may develop arthritis that makes movement painful and may rob the cat of even the slightest desire to walk to a litter box. In these cases, you should consider adding a litter box closer to where the cat spends most of her time. And perhaps get her a litter box with lower sides, or build a ramp around it so it is easier for her to enter.

The litter box as culprit

Defecation problems are much rarer than problems with inappropriate urination. If there is no medical problem, they are likely to result from a problem with the litter or the litter box.

Sometimes the problem is placement of the box. Cats do not like their food and their wastes in close proximity. They prefer very clean kitty boxes and some privacy, some going so far as not to share a box with another cat. They are also particular about the type of litter used and how much of it is present in the box. When you have several cats, it often is difficult to satisfy all of them. One may like a box with a top and small entrance, while another wants a box that is totally open so that he may escape from the other cats in the house. Another cat may not like to use nonclumping litter. One cat may not like the location of the box and so on. And each cat may manifest his or her displeasure by urinating or defecating someplace where he or she should not.

Outdoor cats

If you have a free-ranging cat accustomed to roaming outside, his natural tendency to eliminate outside of his core area in which he lives and not cover his feces may irk neighbors. Because this behavior cannot be effectively changed in an outdoor cat, you may have to resort to making him an indoor cat.

Stress

Environmental stresses

A cat who moves into a new home, notes a change in the owner's schedule or interactions with her, or suddenly has to contend with a new cat, dog, or person in the house, may respond with inappropriate elimination. While the cat owner often cannot change circumstances so the cat will return to her old routine, understanding the possible effects of these changes on the cat can help make the transition a little smoother.

Location, location, location

When deciding where to place the litter box, the cat owner must consider the cat's perspective, since he will be the one using it. Most cats prefer a quiet, easily accessible spot in which to eliminate. Thus, locating the box in a heavily trafficked area, such as a laundry room or kitchen, may be convenient for the owner, but it may cause the cat to seek a more suitable, private site. One owner moved her cats' litter box from the floor to a dresser to prevent her dog from getting into the litter. Subsequently, one of the cats stopped using it. Think of the litter box in terms of your own bathroom. If you wouldn't want your toilet in that location, consider that Felix may not want his there, either.

Emotional states

Emotional upsets can lead to inappropriate urination or defecation. Stress can result from many different sources: a move, a change in the inhabitants of the household (e.g., addition of a dog, a child, a grandparent), a change in schedule, or even refurnishing the house. If you can identify the cause of stress, you may be able to minimize its effects. If nothing helps, a visit to the veterinarian is in order. The cat may require treatment with behavior-modifying medications or may require behavioral therapy and retraining.

Encouraging the Cat to Use the Litter Box

An unpleasant experience at the litter pan may make a cat avoid it. Painful defecation, medicating a cat while she's in the pan, items falling off the shelf onto a cat in the pan below, or other untoward events may be associated in the cat's mind with the litter box. To make sure your cat begins to use the litter box again, you may have to retrain her.

Start by limiting the cat to one room of the house, preferably a room with no rugs or upholstered furniture. Put the litter box in the room and feed the cat on the opposite side of the room. If the cat uses the litter box regularly, gradually allow her more access to your home. Eventually, you will be able to move the litter box to its appropriate location and the cat can go back to having free run of the house. (See pages 41–43 for more information on how to encourage your cat to use the litter box.)

Excrement Marking

It is rare for cats to use feces for scent-marking, although it is not unheard of. A dominant feral cat may leave feces uncovered in conspicuous places, especially along trails of good hunting areas. Don't expect that this is the reason your cat leaves you a package prominently displayed on the dining room table. He may be telling you something (about his litter box or social situation), or simply indicating his presence.

How to Resolve Problems—Spraying

What to Do

The first step in resolving a problem with spraying is to address the condition that may be triggering it, such as overcrowding or exposure to unaltered tomcats. If you cannot effectively eliminate the stimulus, or the cat continues to spray, you can try to change your cat's response to the triggering event. Applying an unpleasant-smelling repellent can divert the cat from his prime targets, since the cat typically sniffs an object before he sprays it. While this tactic may save your drapes or walls from further onslaughts, it may only redirect the cat to seek some other object in the area on which to spray.

Neutering Helps

Neutering your tomcat or queen is strongly advised to reduce their drive to mark their territory. Spraying behavior is enhanced by postpubertal male sex hormones, making castration an effective choice. If you castrate your tomcat before he is a year old, he is unlikely to spray. (However, there is a 10 percent rate of recurrence in older cats.) If your male is not castrated while still young, the result is more variable, although 87 percent of older males abandon the habit of spraying after castration. Along with changes in spraying come reductions in roaming and sexually related fighting. Six hours after the procedure, there is a marked reduction in the level of testosterone in the blood. Interestingly, 78 percent of cats will stop spraying soon after the procedure, while in another 9 percent, these changes occur more gradually over a period of a few months. The presence of unspayed females in the household will increase even the neutered male's urge to spray.

Social Stress

Social stress may be a factor in spraying problems. The best solution is to reduce the number of cats in the household. Unfortunately, it is hard to find homes for adult cats, and the owners usually opt to keep all of their cats. The environment created by a multicat household may cause many of the spraying cats to require behavior-modifying medications.

Feliway

Another way to reduce spraying is to release a synthetic feline cheek gland secretion, Feliway® (sold by Abbott Laboratories and available from veterinarians), in the cat's favorite spraying spots. The goal here is to replace one mark—urine—for another—cheek gland secretion—so that the spraying cat might be enticed by the synthetic cheek gland spray to respond in kind.

Behavior-Modifying Medications

Behavior-modifying medications can be successful when you do not want to have the cat castrated or spayed, when castration is unsuccessful, or in ovariohysterectomized (spayed) females. Any of these medications will need to be prescribed by your veterinarian, following a consultation on the cat's spraying history. They should be used with caution and under a veterinarian's care. Doses to cats must be carefully adjusted because the feline liver is not as effective in detoxifying drugs as the human or canine liver. Such medications as clomipramine (Clomicalm®), amitriptyline (Elavil®), buspirone (BuSpar®), diazepam (Valium®), paroxetine (Paxil®), or synthetic progestins (Depo-Provera®, Ovaban®, or Megase®) can suppress spraying, most likely because they help to decrease anxiety, which can trigger the behavior. Some of these drugs, such as the progestins and occasionally diazepam, can have serious side effects.

Buspirone, an antianxiety medication, and amitriptyline, an antidepressant, prove helpful in about 60 percent of the cases. Diazepam (Valium) is an antianxiety tranquilizer that is particularly useful if housesoiling is stress-related. It is more effective than hormonal therapy for females and for cats living in multicat households. Because liver poisoning has recently been identified as a side effect in some cats, your cat should first undergo certain blood tests before diazepam is given, then be monitored closely in consultation with your veterinarian while this drug is being administered.

With any of the behavior-modifying medications discussed, the best approach is to first remove the stressor in the cat's environment, either before or when the treatment begins. The drugs work best as temporary stress-relievers.

Behavioral Modification

Another form of therapy that can prove useful in countering spraying is behavioral modification. Here, timing is critical. The cat owner can use a water pistol, a remotely controlled plant sprayer, a noise, a light flash, or a thrown object to deter a cat from spraying. Keep in mind that this tactic must start as soon as the cat begins to spray and must be used consistently. Alternatively, you can hang strips of aluminum foil on the target object so that when they are sprayed, they make noise and/or reflect the spray, discouraging the cat from spraying. Ironically, this last tactic was successful in a few cases because the cat became distracted by playing with the foil. In fact, some cats learn to prefer spraying on the foil.

Surgical Intervention

Cats appear to recognize other cats by smell. Because the cat's sense of smell and his behavior are connected, the cat owner can opt for surgical intervention. One procedure, called olfactory tractotomy, severs the connection between the olfactory bulb (the part of the brain responsible for the sense of smell) and the rest of the brain. This procedure successfully eliminates spraying in most females and half the males who spray, and reportedly, it does not adversely affect appetite and food intake. A more complicated procedure is to create brain lesions surgically. While it also eliminates spraying, unlike olfactory tractotomy, it requires specialized equipment and training—and it is an extreme treatment. Neurosurgical intervention to solve any feline behavioral problem is extreme and should only be considered in concert with veterinary advice—and only as a last resort.

How to Resolve Problems— Inappropriate Urination and Defecation

Litter Hygiene

We can't say it enough: Trying to encourage the cat to consistently use the litter box requires that you make the box as attractive to the cat as possible. Cleanliness and appropriate location are essential. The following tips will help keep the kitty box inviting:

- The problems cat owners experience with cats who make mistakes and don't use the boxes may be related to a quality of the box itself. Try boxes of different shapes or sizes.

- Select a litter box made of easily washable plastic or other nonabsorbent material. It must be large enough for your cat to use comfortably—at least 14" by 18" by 4" deep.

- Place the box in a quiet, out-of-the-way spot.

- Make sure you have enough pans. A cat sleeping on the third floor of the house may not want to walk down to the basement to use the litter box. There should be a box per floor in a multistory house. In a multicat household, there should be a box per cat plus one.

- For adult cats, use clumping litter, since most cats prefer the texture. It also facilitates cleanup by gathering into a ball when urine comes in contact with it. Avoid clumping litter for very young kittens, however, as it may be dangerous for them if ingested. (Also avoid it if you have dogs who snack in the litter box.)

- Do not use litter containing a highly perfumed deodorant. Although the perfume may mask the urine odor, your cat is likely to hate it and reject the box. Avoid using strongly perfumed cleaning products; the cat may not like them and may refuse to use the box.

- When you change types of litter, do so gradually so the cat becomes used to the new litter. Be sure one pan containing the original litter is present for the first few days in case the cat doesn't like the new one.

- Strain clumping litter daily and replenish the litter as needed; if you use nonclumping litter, you must discard it completely if the cat's problem is soiling.

- Do not stir soiled litter, as stirring only spreads the odor.

- At least once a week, change the litter completely and wash the box with a mild detergent and hot water (and wash your hands thoroughly after completing the task). Never use household or commercial cleaning agents containing dangerous ingredients such as phenol. However, dilute solutions of chlorine bleach are safe to use.

- When you rinse the box, use vinegar to neutralize residual urine odor.

- Do not use cleaning products containing ammonia, because they will intensify the urine odor.

- Some cats hate plastic litter pan liners; they either don't like the smell of the plastic or they object to the way they feel to their feet. Discontinue their use if your cat fails to use the box routinely.

- If your cat still insists on urinating or defecating outside the box, con-

Clumping Litter

Although there is some anecdotal evidence of kittens dying from ingesting clumping litter, there is little or no scientific evidence to support this. Nevertheless, as a precaution, don't use clumping litter for very young kittens. You may also prefer not to use clumping litter if your dog "snacks" from the litter box (a habit that can be broken by using a covered litter box and turning the opening so that the cat can get in but the dog cannot get his snout in there).

sult your veterinarian, as this could signify behavioral or physical problems.

Practicing the Art of Dissuasion

In addition to keeping the kitty box fresh, you must also attempt to dissuade the cat from frequenting areas outside the box. Thus, it is important to thoroughly clean any soiled areas. Once the cat associates even a mild odor of urine or feces with an area, that area becomes attractive and the cat is apt to soil near it again. When urine is exposed to air, environmental bacteria break down the nitrogen-containing components of the urine, producing an acrid, ammonialike smell. Possible choices of cleaning products include carbonated soda water, soapy water with a vinegar-water rinse, or any of the many commercial products. Many of the odor-removing products sold in pet supply stores, by catalog, or even in supermarkets are effective. Buy a number of brands and pick the one that seems to work the best without damaging the surface you're cleaning. Commercial preparations containing enzymes—but not ammonia—are the best bet for this job.

Another approach that has been successful is to use food bowls or a kitty box as deterrents by placing them in areas in which the cat usually urinates. Alternatively, Fluffy may benefit from temporary confinement within a small room equipped with food, water, a litter pan, and, perhaps, some toys to minimize environmental stresses (see box on Encouraging, page 37).

The Kitty Litter Revolution

Before cat litter was invented, the family cat went outdoors to do his business. But 50 years ago, Edward Lowe invented Kitty Litter®, and that changed the relationship between humans and their cats. Cats no longer needed to go outdoors to eliminate, but could do so in a place just for themselves in the house. Clay litter is not the only litter material on the market, although it is the most commonly used litter material. There now are a variety of litters based on grass, grain, recycled paper, corncobs, and citrus pulp, among other products.

If your cat soiled just after you switched litter material, you can reintroduce the original litter material to see if that helps. If you are not sure of your cat's preference for litter type, you might offer several types of material in different litter boxes. A selection such as sand or soil, alfalfa pellets, clay (scented and unscented), sawdust, paper, wheat, or corncobs can help bypass your cat's aversion to a specific substance. Most cats prefer the fine particles that comprise clumping litter. For cats who have had access to the outdoors, mixing soil with the litter can be helpful.

Some cats prefer a more pliable material than the plastic interior of a litter box to scratch while making burying movements. Thus, they may be coaxed to use the litter box if you position a small piece of carpeting in the litter box or attach it to the rim.

Finally, keep in mind that cats are creatures of habit; relatively minor changes can alter their behavior Their keen faculties process sight, smell, shape—and, to some degree, color—as daily stimuli that evoke either positive or negative responses.

Litter Box Containers

As previously mentioned, cat owners should put out at least one box per cat (preferably more) with boxes located on every floor if you live in a multistory house. This is especially important in multicat households where one cat may be prevented from using a certain litter box by another cat, or a cat may prefer not to eliminate in the same area as another. Some cats use one box exclusively for defecation and another for urination, while other cats just prefer larger boxes. For cats who like to perch on the edge of the box, a platform built around the rim can make them more comfortable. Providing boxes of different sizes and types—both covered and uncovered—in several locations can be a tremendous help in eliminating bad habits.

Controlling Odor

Dr. Richards, of Cornell's Feline Health Center, suggests that the careful choice, placement, and management of a cat's litter box will help to control any odor problem. "If a cat rejects his litter box, he's going to urinate or defecate elsewhere," Dr. Richards points out, "and you're going to have the odor." The cat is looking for a box that is accessible, clean, and affords him a little privacy.

One product that might fit the bill is a standard-sized plastic litter box with a hood. The cat enters through a flap or opening and, surrounded by the darkness inside, has all the privacy he could want. But remember to clean the box often because it traps odors inside, and don't be disappointed if your cat hates this box—some cats do.

Retraining Strategies

Despite your efforts to decrease your cat's stress levels, you may still have to retrain some recalcitrant cats to use the litter box. There are a number of approaches to use. Confining the cat to a small room or a cage with a litter box in it can help: Cats are reluctant to eliminate in a confined area because they do not like to soil their sleeping quarters. When the cat begins to use the litter box consistently again, you may allow her access to other areas of the house.

Another approach is to place the litter box on top of the cat's favorite elimination site, and then gradually move it to a more desirable location. Or you might try using an approach akin to one used for house-training dogs: As soon as the cat awakens in the morning, bring her to the litter box and praise her for using it.

If you are up for a challenge, you might consider training the cat to eliminate on command. In this case, you must become aware of the times the

---

Different Litters for Different Cats

Nonspraying elimination should be treated by changing the characteristics of the litter. Some cats like deep litter; others, shallow. Vary the depth of litter within the box so the cat can "vote" by using the depth he prefers. Different types of litter should be presented. The majority of cats prefer clumping litter because it is made of fine particles similar to sand. Provide one box for urine and another for feces. Try placing litter boxes in several locations. You might try substituting a tray for a box or a covered litter pan for an open one, or vice versa cat usually eliminates and call the cat to the litter box at those times. Encourage her to eliminate by stirring the (clean) litter, then praise her for eliminating. Toilet training the cat may also relieve the problem. There are several books on the market that explain how to toilet train a cat. Check with Direct Book Service (Wenatchee, Washington) on the Web at www.dogandcatbooks.com or call them at 1-800-776-2665.

Defecation problems should also be treated by changing the litter type or the location of the box. A low-sided box or tray is often successful.

Repellents

Repellents may be effective in discouraging a cat from eliminating in a particular area, but the drawback is that the cat usually will choose another area. If you wish to try a repellent, choose a citrus-scented air freshener or strongly scented soap for the best results. Applying it to your cat's favorite elimination targets should discourage her from urinating at those sites. The downside, however, is that she is likely to shift her attention to another, untampered-with spot in the house.

Given the limited utility of repellents in keeping kitty away from urinating on inappropriate objects, the best strategy may be to guide her toward the litter box by making it more enticing. Of course, as we reemphasize, it is important to keep the box as clean as possible and ensure that it is located in an attractive place for the cat. In conjunction, you should erase all traces of soiling in inappropriate spots so as not to persuade her to return to those sites.

Outdoors?

If all else fails and your cat has worn out her welcome in the home with her spraying or indiscriminate urinating, a last resort may be to extend her time spent outdoors. The trick here is to keep on feeding her at regular intervals to maintain her

---

Do Not Punish

Punishing your cat is not a good idea: Instead of correcting the behavior, physical or harsh vocal punishment will teach your cat to avoid or fear you. The unwanted behavior will continue—only not in your presence—and if the behavior is triggered by stress, punishing will compound the stress. Other strategies to correct the cat's behavior are usually more effective, without risking destroying the bond established between you and your feline companion.

bond to you. This method encourages her to eliminate outside by default; thus, when you readmit her inside for brief periods, she won't soil your home. Keep in mind, though, that cats face a number of risks outside of the home, including disease, injury, and even death. For this reason, the Cornell University College of Veterinary Medicine does not recommend that cats be allowed outdoors.

For the Cat Who's Never Been Litter Box Trained—It Takes Patience

What if your cat has never taken to using a litter box? This history poses a much greater challenge in trying to get him to change his behavior at this stage of his life. Training a cat to use a litter box involves restricting him to a cage with a shelf whose entire floor is covered with cat litter. You then gradually give him more freedom in one room, leaving the cage floor as a litter box and the door open. Next, remove the cage, but leave the floor as a litter box. Finally, substitute a litter box for the cage floor. When he is able to use his litter box exclusively for another week, he can graduate to other areas of the house.

Summary

Now you have the basis for understanding that the wide array of behaviors your cat displays is often a manifestation of her basic feline nature. What should also be evident by now is that, given the restraints of a household, normal cat behaviors such as scent-marking or scratching can be ruinous to your home and peace of mind. Fortunately, by understanding the basis for some of these behaviors and applying the strategies outlined in this report, the cat owner stands a good chance of ameliorating—or even abolishing—objectionable behaviors. At the very least, you may learn to be more tolerant of some of them.

Cat owners tend to be very curious about how other cat owners handle their feline friends. Thus, it is relatively easy to strike up a conversation with a fellow ailurophile in the pet food aisle of the supermarket. After the owners finish the complaints about their cat's extreme finickiness about his or her diet, the next topic seems to be how much furniture each cat has destroyed. No one ever believes the owner who says her precious Fuzzball has never destroyed a thing, not anything at all. It's hard to believe them as you tally up the number of chairs and sofas destroyed by clawing, the carpets saturated with urine, and the important papers shredded. Sometimes you think you are the only person in the world whose cat misbehaves. As this report indicates, you are not alone. So many cats do bad things that the numbers are staggering. And the solution is to try to prevent the misbehavior or tolerate it and note that it's a price you must pay for feline companionship.

Removing the triggers or redirecting the cat to more acceptable outlets through behavioral modification will restore harmony in the household. Addressing the cat's fundamental needs—such as keeping a scrupulously clean, well-placed litter box, providing a scratching post to satisfy clawing and grooming needs, and being sensitive to the cat's perspective when effecting household changes—will preserve an intact, fresh-smelling home and encourage a satisfying relationship with your feline companion.

Caring for a cat can be a wonderful and rewarding experience. But, as with any relationship, conflicts can arise. While humans and cats cannot be said to speak the same precise language, a little understanding of feline behavior and communication will do wonders to help cue us into their perception of the world. If we take the time to find out what it is they want to tell us, and act on that information to help solve their problems—either by ourselves or by taking them for a consultation with a veterinarian—then we will be rewarded by the joy and fulfillment that a harmonious cat-owner relationship can bring. In the end, everyone benefits from love, especially when an owner expresses that love by providing his or her cat with thoughtful and informed health care.

Recommended Resources on Cat Behavior

The following books are highly recommended for those who want to learn more about cat behavior:

Ackerman, L., compiler. *Cat Behavior and Training.* Neptune City, New Jersey: T.F.H. Publications, Inc., 1996.

Askew, H.R. *Treatment of Behavior Problems in Dogs and Cats: A Guide for the Small Animal Veterinarian.* Oxford, U.K.: Blackwell Science, 1996.

Beaver, B.V. *Feline Behavior: A Guide for Veterinarians.* Philadelphia, Pennsylvania: W.B. Saunders and Company, 1992.

Beaver, B.V. *The Veterinarian's Encyclopedia of Animal Behavior.* Ames, Iowa: Iowa State University Press, 1994.

Hart, B.L., Hart, L.A. *Canine and Feline Behavioral Therapy.* Philadelphia, Pennsylvania: Lea & Febiger, 1985.

Houpt, K.A. *Domestic Animal Behavior for Veterinarians and Animal Scientists.* Ames, Iowa: Iowa State University Press, 1998.

Milani, M.M. *The Body Language and Emotion of Cats.* New York: Quill, William Morrow, 1987.

Morris, D. *Cat World: A Feline Encyclopedia.* New York: Penguin Reference, 1997.

Siegal, M., ed. *The Cornell Book of Cats,* 2nd Edit. New York: Villard Books, 1997. [Order this book directly from the Cornell Feline Health Center. Call 1-607-253-3414 for more information.]

Tabor, R. *Understanding Cats: Their History, Nature, and Behavior.* Pleasantville, New York: Reader's Digest, 1997.

Turner, D.C., Bateson, P. *The Domestic Cat.* Cambridge, U.K.: Cambridge University Press, 1988.

THE WELL-BEHAVED CAT: HOW TO CHANGE YOUR CAT'S BAD HABITS

To order additional copies of *The Well Behaved Cat: How to Change Your Cat's Bad Habits,* **please call toll-free: 1-800-571-1555.**

Please address inquiries for bulk orders and permission to reproduce selections from this special report to: Torstar Publications, 99 Hawley Lane, Suite 1440, Stratford, CT 06614.